CW00551030

Format Your Book

Format Your Book

How to Format your manuscript for Amazon using Microsoft Word!

By Mark Stattelman

Copyright © 2020 Mark Stattelman
All Rights Reserved

ISBN-13:9798652084516

Table of Contents

Why Do it Myself?

You might ask . . .

This is a very good question, and one a lot of people ask. You can obviously just pay someone else to format your book. Most writers would rather just write the book. True. I was the same way. You have to make the choice. People either have time or money to invest . . .

You might ask another question to help you figure it out.

How much does it cost to pay someone else to do it? I've seen the price as low as $10 on fiverr. And I've seen it for about $50. Just remember, you get what you pay for. And what about revisions? You will have errors, such as typos, and other mistakes, even after the editing process; Well, unless you live in a perfect world. Maybe you are able to edit the file they send you (I'm guessing that you can?) I simply don't know because I've never used these services. Do these people charge you for revisions if you change your mind about other things?

The bigger question that has to be considered is whether this is going to be a one-off? Are you only going to write one book? If you are only going to write one book, then paying someone might be the better option.

This is book number eleven for me (I've got two under a pseudonym), and I also have two more in the pipeline and another five in various stages. But, let's just consider the eleven. At $50 a pop (I'm not sure I would trust anyone to do it for less, but that's just me), that's $550. I believe I would rather hang on to that chunk of change. Add the next two books onto this and that's $650. For $650 I can get two Very Nice book covers done on 99Designs.

Okay, so you have to decide. I tend to agree with the old adage of whether feeding a man one meal, or teaching him how to fish is the better option. I'm gonna go with the latter. I'm here to teach you how to fish, so to speak.

So, with a little bit of time and effort you'll be all set. You can probably read this book over in an afternoon; or work with it over a weekend to format your own book. *Both ebook and paperback!*

More importantly, I'm going to point out the "trouble spots" and help you work through them. I've tried to make all of the information very clear and concise, with details on exactly what to do to accomplish each specific thing. Furthermore, I have things all laid out in a way for you to go directly to the section you need.

You can just do the short section, which simply tells you the specific keys to use or buttons to click to get the job done; Or you can read through the more detailed section to accomplish what you need.

It took me three weeks of struggling, trying to figure things out. I'm trying to make it so you don't have to take that long, or go through all the hassle. I couldn't really find much specific help out there at the time I was trying to figure out how to format my first couple of books. I did find out what the trouble spots were, finally, but with no real idea how to fix things. It took me a while to figure it out. I sincerely hope this book helps you.

I will say that I only give instructions on things I've actually used and done.

I used Microsoft Word 2019 (and also Kindle Create, but I'll explain that later), on a Windows pc.

If you have a Mac, then I'm guessing you are pretty savvy regarding which keys match up to the windows pc keys. I only know that you hit Cmd in place of Ctrl, in some instances, or perhaps all instances. I am totally ignorant on that aspect, so I don't address Macs. Perhaps in a later edition of the book I can remedy things in that regard.

Also, I've never published a book with photos, so I won't address that (bleed or no bleed), etc.

I would say "good luck" but you don't need it, because you'll have the know-how with this book.

Just a note: At the time of this book's current update (June 2023) I have Formatted and Published nineteen books (15 books under my own name and 4 books under a pseudonym), and am working on number twenty and twenty-one. I didn't bother to change/update the number of books I mentioned in the intro to this book, explaining how much money you would save by formatting your own books because, the point remains valid regardless of the number of books. The more books published only emphasizes the point. You save more money by doing the formatting yourself rather than hiring it out.

This book is for absolute beginners, or those with some skills in Word, who just need to find out specific things on how to format their manuscript for upload to Amazon.

What You Need to Know

First things first:

You'll have to decide on these things:
1) Trim size
2) Margins
3) Font style and Font size
4) Line Spacing

Other Important info:

(Most of the following pertains to fiction only. Nonfiction sometimes)

1) You'll have to have an even page count at the end of your manuscript. This is an Amazon submission rule.
So, if you come to the end of your book and have an odd page number, add a page (or rather, a section break).

2) Every chapter (If your book is a novel) should start on an odd page.

3) The Chapter heading should start about half-way down the middle of the page.

4) No header on page where chapter begins.

5) No page number on page where chapter begins.

6) If previous chapter ends on odd page, add a blank page (two section breaks).

7) No headers or page numbers on blank pages.

The Most Important Things to Remember:
(The trouble spots)
These are the nightmarish things that will have you pulling your hair out and losing sleep if you don't get a handle on them.

1) The **"link to previous"** button is your enemy! This will be your biggest nightmare.

2) Always use **section breaks** rather than page breaks. Put a section break after every chapter.

Now don't worry!
I'm here to walk you through all of it.

How to think about a Word document

It helps to think of your Word document as a length of chain. This might sound strange at first, but when it comes to using the **Link to Previous** button, thinking along these lines makes it all easier to understand.

So, if the whole document is a length of chain, then you can imagine each page of the document as being an individual link of that chain. Each page in Word is, in fact, linked all the way through the document from beginning to end.

Okay, but you want to section things off into chapters, right? Or stories (if you—as I often do—write books of short stories).

Why would you want to section things off? Well, most often you want to do this when working with Headers and Footers (Footers are simply page numbers in my books). You might want the title for whatever story the reader is reading to be listed at the top of the page (a Header). If you leave everything linked together in one long chain, when you add the Header title for one story Word will automatically add that Header/Title all the way through the chain (book). You will end up with one story title, or Header displayed for stories that actually have totally different titles.

If you are writing a novel, then this won't matter so much. You'll probably, if you so choose, have your name as a Header on one page (even pages) and your book's title on the opposite page (odd pages) alternating all the way through the book.

If you are writing a work of nonfiction, you might want to do different things in different areas of the book. You will want different sections covering different topics or have various sub sections.

So, yes, you'll need to "Unlink" your pages at various spots.

Another example is separating front matter of your book from the main text or body of the manuscript. For instance, I unlink each and every page of my front matter, even from each other. I use roman numerals (i, ii iii, iv . . .) for the page numbers in my front matter (even if the numbers are not visible on the page) and then start with regular (Arabic) number one (1) and so on for the regular text starting with the first page of chapter, or story one (unless I have a

Prologue, in which case I generally start page one there).

I explain all of this (how to add Headers and page numbers) in more detail in the **Header and Footer** section and the **To Add Page Numbers** section of the book. To get to all of the Header and Footer tools, just double click in the top or bottom margin areas of any open Word document.

Also, get used to adding section breaks at the end of each chapter, story, or section of your manuscript. This will be explained in the **Adding Section Breaks** section.

So, thinking of the manuscript as being a length of chain, which you then section off, helps. At least it helped me to get a handle on understanding the Link to Previous button. If I have a manuscript of 100 pages and one of the chapters starts on page 31 and ends on page 40, I will first put a section break at the bottom of the text on page 40. Then, on page 41 I will click in the top margin to bring up the Header and Footer tools and then click the **Link to Previous** button to remove the link (if the button is high-lighted). Then I'll move to the bottom margin and do the same. After this, I'll go back to page 31 and unlink page 31 from page 30. And I'll most likely check the Different First page box. I just watch to make sure the Link to Previous button doesn't activate again. If so, I click that button again to un-highlight it.

You'll have to play around a bit to get used to all of this, of course. But as long as you keep the chain analogy in mind it should help in understanding how it all works. I'm sure Microsoft has some document out there explaining the details, but God only knows where to find it. I struggled for a good long while to figure things out; but once I started thinking of the chain analogy everything sort of made a little more sense. The analogy seems simplistic, but also clarifying. I hope it helps you as well.

Let's Get Started

I'm assuming that you have a manuscript, or at least the start of a manuscript. Possibly you have no more than just a few chapters, maybe just a couple. That is okay. Whatever you have so far is fine. Often it is easier to just work with a few chapters, or the start of your book just to set things up. You might feel a little overwhelmed with all of it being right there. So, maybe, if you have a complete novel, just copy and paste the first few chapters into a new document. You can set up your trim size and margins, etc., with a blank document, but it is easier, or more visible and understandable if you can watch text shift into place. You can work on just a few chapters for a trial run-through, just to play around and become familiar with the layout of things . . . Or, you can just work directly on your book. If you want to jump in and work directly on your manuscript that's fine. If so, you can skip the part about opening Word and a new blank document. You probably have a copy of the whole manuscript tucked away somewhere anyway, right? Just in case things get too crazy. What could possibly go wrong? Just kidding.

Open Word.

Click on **File**.

Click on **New.**

Click on **Blank Document**.

If you have some text, a document ready to work with (as in *not* a blank document), use that if you want. Or you can right-click on some text, select it and click **Copy (CTRL+C can be used if you have the text highlighted); then Paste (CTRL+V) the text into the blank document.**

Here is where you should decide which is easier: Whether to add a series of section breaks (Under Layout tab, click Breaks and then Next Page) to leave plenty of blank pages (6 to 8 pages), room enough for your front matter. You can do this before you Copy and Paste the document in place into the new blank document. It is totally up to you as to which way you do this. You can always come back and add the pages later and type in all of the front matter then. See section on **Front Matter and formatting page numbers**.

Why do you need six to eight pages?

Well, you have the following (generally speaking) make up of front matter:
Half Title page (Just the title, usually)
Blank page
Title page (The title, subtitle, and by line—which is your author name)
Copyright page (on back of Title page)
Dedication page (if you want one)
Blank page
Table of Contents

You also might have a note to reader or a Prelude or Prologue. The blank pages are basically spacers so that the pages with information will be on the right-hand side facing the reader. The only information on the "back" of a page will be the copyright info, which is on the back of the Title page.

Ok, so here is what we are looking at at this point. Your screen should be showing the following, provided you have Microsoft Word opened up and ready to go.
At the top of the screen, in blue, you've got tabs showing:

File | Home | Insert | Design | Layout | References | Mailings | Review | View | Help |

I believe Microsoft calls this a ribbon. Don't know why they started calling it that, but anyway . . .

To Set Trim Size:

The brief version:

Click on **Layout**
Click on **Size**
Click on **More Paper Sizes**
Change **Width** and **Height** to desired sizes
Apply to **Whole Document**

The detailed walkthrough:

So, at the top of the screen you should see the labels listed just as I showed you above. If you look, you'll see that the fifth button over from left-hand side is called **Layout**. That's the one you want.
Click on it.
You'll see buttons/Icons (pictures) below the blue. These will be in white (sort of). You want to click on the third icon from the left. It looks like a piece of paper with the top right corner folded down. **Size** is the label below the icon. Here is where we are going to set the trim size for your book.
So, what is trim size? It is just the height and width you want your book to be. Pick up any book you have

lying around and grab a ruler. Measure from the top of the cover to the bottom of the cover. This is height. Now measure the cover from side to side. This is the width. Pretty obvious, right? Your book is cut out of paper, so I'm assuming that is where the word *trim* comes from, and they have to know what size to trim it to. And the printing on the pages has to remain within these bounds . . .

If you are having trouble deciding on the size you want, it is okay. You can always change the size before you upload anything.

Personally, I usually use **5" by 8"** which is, I believe, the smallest size Amazon allows.

So, you've clicked on the **Siz**e button. What happened? You should see a drop-down list. Go to the bottom of the list where it reads "**More Paper Sizes . . .**," and click on that. You should see a dialog box (labelled Page Setup at top) pop up where you will see *paper size:* You can adjust the width and height in the boxes below this, either using the arrow keys, or by typing in the boxes. Go ahead and change these now. **Change the width to 5"** and the **height to 8"**. If you have already decided on your own to use a different size that is fine, of course. You might prefer

6" by 9" or whatever. Check the Amazon website to see the sizes they allow.

Now, further down in this dialog box, and at the bottom, you should see where it says

apply to: use the drop-down arrow to change the box to read *whole document*. . .

Okay, now look up at the top of the dialog box and you will see three tabs: **Margins**, **Paper**, **Layout**. You'll notice that the Paper tab is highlighted. That is where you are now. You want to now click on the tab to the left of Paper. This is the **Margins** tab. Click on it. Or . . . you can click OK to save your selections and close box. If you close out, then you can do the following:

To Set Margins:

The brief version:

Click on **Layout**
Click on **Margins**
Click on **Custom Margins** . . .
Change Multiple Pages: Normal to **Mirror Margins**

Change Top, Bottom, Outside, and Inside margins, but Do Not change Gutter.
Actually, Top and Bottom are probably ok at 1"

The detailed Walkthrough:

Click on **Layout** (fifth button from left at top of screen), then just below this "ribbon" you'll see the same row of icons that had the Size icon. The first button is the **Margins** icon. Click on this and go to bottom of list where you see *custom margins* and click on that. Here you will see the same dialog box (labelled page setup at the top) that has the three tabs: Margins, Paper, Layout. If you didn't move, or close out the box, from when we set the paper size (trim size), then you are already here.
Okay, *the very **first** thing you need to do* in this box, once you have the Margins tab highlighted is to go down to where it says, **Multiple Pages:** In the box to the right it should say Normal. You want to use the drop-down arrow to change this to **Mirror Margins.**
Now you want to look at the bottom of box where it says **apply to:** and if it doesn't already say whole document, change this (same as you did in paper tab

section) to **whole document**. If you changed it when you set trim size, it is probably already correct. Now go back up to the top of the box where you have the margins listed. You can change these as you see fit; however, it is usually best to leave the **gutter** settings as they are.

These are the settings I usually use for margins (feel free to experiment and see what is best for you):

Top: 1"   **Bottom: 1"**
Inside: .65"   **Outside: .5"**

The inside margin is usually set larger than the outside, because this is where the pages of the book are bound together. You want enough space on the inside so the reader can read the text easily. The text needs to be far enough away from the binding so the reader can hold the book casually and not have to smash it flat to try and see the text.

And don't panic if your text looks "snakey" on your computer screen with your pages stacked one on top of the other and running down the screen. The text will appear closer to the left side of one page and then be closer to the right side on the next page down. This is normal (provided you have the mirror margins box checked), and due to the inside margin being larger. Imagine the pages being side by side in a book, with the wider margins meeting in the middle. The shift in text might just be a subtle difference depending on how big the difference is between the outside and inside margins

.

To Set Font Style and Font Size:

On **Home** Tab
Look in **Font** section
Click on drop-down arrow in **font name** box to change name of font to another font on the list. To the right of this you have the drop-down box and arrow to change the **font size**.

Okay, so this one is pretty simple, right? If you have done any sort of writing, no matter what version of Word, you already know how to do this and where to find the buttons. And maybe you already knew the other. But anyway. . .the more detailed walkthrough

Click on the **Home** tab in ribbon at top of the screen. Just beneath the ribbon you'll see five blocks/areas, with labels at bottom:

Clipboard | **Font** | Paragraph | Styles | Editing

Each one of these blocks has a multitude of symbols and tools within it. For now, we are just concerned with the second one in from left side: **Font**. Within the top of this box you will see two white boxes with drop-down arrows. The first box holds the name of whatever the font is that you are using. The second box (just to the right of the first box) holds the size of that font. You can, of course, use the drop-down arrows to change the font and the size of the font. Pretty simple, right? You just need to decide on which one you like best to use.

Most people, I believe, use **12pt** (size) font. I do. Though I use 16 or 18 for headings, etc.

As far as the style of font, I usually use **Georgia**. But that's apt to change, depending. Various writers will like different font styles. If you are submitting a manuscript the old-fashioned way to a publisher, or a short story to a magazine, or whatever, then you want to use whatever the guidelines are for that publisher. I think the rule of thumb "standard" is Courier, or Times New Roman, for various reasons, which I won't go into here. No need. You are publishing your own book—use what you want! You can, if you don't find a font you like in the normal Word font list, search **Google Fonts,** or one of a ton of other font sites out there. I tend to stick to the basic. Best thing to do is peruse other books in your Genre and figure out what other folks are using. You can definitely get lost down a rabbit hole on this one.

To Set Line Spacing:

The brief version:

On Home tab, find **Paragraph** section (third section in from left beneath blue ribbon)
Click on **tiny arrow in bottom right corner** of Paragraph section.
Look for **spacing section** in dialog box.
Go to **Line Spacing** box and use drop-down arrow to change to single or multiple, etc.
If multiple, then change number in right hand drop-down to read whatever spacing you desire. You can type in the number.

The detailed walkthrough:

Click the Home tab on the ribbon if you aren't still on it from the last section. This is the same one with the five blocks with labels at the bottom: Clipboard, Font, Paragraph . . .

We want the third block in from the left (just to the right of the font section): **Paragraph**

There is a small, diagonally pointing arrow in the bottom right-hand corner of this box. Click on it. You'll see a **paragraph** dialog box spring open. Now, there are several ways to get to this box. You can also just right-click if you are on a page of text (same as you do for the copy and paste commands, only you would go to the paragraph label and click on it instead of copy or paste.)

You will see two tabs at the top of the box. You want the left-hand tab: Indents and Spacing (which should already be displayed). Below this you will see four sections:

General, Indentation, Spacing, and Preview. You want the section labelled **Spacing.**

Look in the right-hand side of this section and you will see two drop-down boxes, one labelled **Line Spacing**, and the other labelled **At.** This is what we are looking for.

Now, I'm thinking most people probably set the line spacing at **Single** (using the drop-down arrows). I, however, use **Multiple** and then change the **At:** to read **1.25** (though I'm trying **1.20** for this book.

This, of course is just the amount of space you have between your lines of text (hence the name of the label). I, due to eyesight/eye strain issues, prefer to have more space between my lines. At first when I used it and got my first proof of the first book, I thought Oh my God, it looks like a large print book. This kind of freaked me out. I'm not that blind.

This setting does give my books sort of a light and breezy feel while reading. The only problem there is, is that people might feel like they aren't getting enough text/material; Not true! If the reader gets to the end and thinks about it, there was plenty of material presented. A lot of my books are Short Story compilations; and I do put enough stories in the books to give an entertaining ride, one that is lengthy enough. No one has really complained. But I'm thinking of experimenting, and maybe dropping down to 1.10 eventually.

As I'm writing, I generally keep the line spacing setting at double space, as it is less of a strain on the eyes. On rare occasions I'll bump the font size to 14pt. But the final format setting for line spacing is (for me) normally 1.25. This is unless I'm just doing a draft, or submitting something to a publisher, which is usually (if rules still hold) double spaced text (a draft). But I digress.

Back to the matter at hand:

In the **Spacing** section, while we're still here, take note of the left-hand side of this section block. Here you will see **Before**, and **After** drop-downs. We will return to this section and use these later. Remember how I said the Chapter beginnings need to be halfway down the page? Well that's where the *before* and *after* side of this section comes in handy.

Okay, so that pretty much covers the *first things first* points. Now let's move on to the other stuff.

Section Two

Using Styles

I have to admit, I don't really use Styles enough. I don't really know a lot about how to use them; but I do know they can come in handy. I know enough to get by. I usually just modify them temporarily. If you are an organized person, you can have your whole book set up with styles, using them as templates. I believe that's how it works.

So, where are they?

Well, if you've got the **Home** tab selected from the ribbon, the **Styles** is the next section over from the paragraph section, just below the ribbon. Remember, we have the Clipboard, the Font, and the Paragraph sections, and then the Styles (which is the one that stretches across the top of the screen—the one with all the varying letters displayed), and then the Editing section. If you can't see the labels right off look at the bottom middle of each section; That's where the label is.

Just about everything we spent time doing in the last section can be set/changed in one fell swoop if we right-click on the **Normal** box (the first one on the left) in the **Styles** section. It all depends on what the default settings are. You can use the default settings if you are happy with the way things look. Just left-click on **Normal**. By the same token, you can modify those default settings to match what we've set up, or to any other setting, by right-clicking on the normal box and then clicking on **Update Normal to Match Selection**, or **Modify . . .**
I generally just temporarily modify.
For typing the chapter titles, I'll often type them out and then keep the text selected and click on **Heading 1** (fourth label from left in styles section). However, this often defaults to Calibri for font and 16pt for size. I then go up and change it. This too can be modified by right-clicking on it, just like with the Normal tab. The great thing about using the **Heading 1** tab for your chapters, or for Short Story titles (which are basically like chapters) is that the heading/chapter title shows up in the **Navigation** pane on the left-hand side of the window. If you have it open. If not, click on **View** button at top of screen and check the Navigation Pane box in the Show

section (to the left of Zoom which is the section with the big magnifying glass).

If you click on Headings in the Navigation pane, you'll see the chapter title, or number (or short story title) listed. In the Navigation pane you have the three headings: Headings, Pages, and Results. I generally flip back and forth between Headings and Pages. And the beauty of using the Styles **Headings** is that at the end of the formatting, once you have everything just as you want it, you can add your table of contents, which just pulls in the headings and adds the page numbers. We'll talk about that later.

So, Styles are handy. You should definitely explore the possibilities. Like I said, I don't really know a lot about them. I tend to use them on a temporary basis. I *can*, however, see the significant potential.

I strongly encourage you to explore Styles! There is *so* much that can be done using this section. So far, I have not explored Styles in this book to any great degree. Perhaps in an updated version of the book I will add a section that goes into more depth on the subject. For now, I confess my ignorance—as I just modify the normal style temporarily.

Adding Section Breaks:

The brief version:

Click on **Layout**
Click on **Breaks**
Click on **Next Page**

The detailed walkthrough:

Remember I said **use section breaks instead of page breaks**. I mean it. The section breaks are much easier to work with than page breaks. You should place them at the end of each chapter, story (if your book is a collection of short stories), or section.

How do you add them?

Well, first I would suggest, turning on the little button that shows everything, all the punctuation marks. You do that by going up to the **Paragraph** section (to the left of the Styles section if you still have the Home tab of the ribbon selected). In the paragraph section look in the upper right-hand corner and you will see what looks like a backwards facing letter P.

There is a name for this symbol, but I can't think of what it is (Pilcrow, maybe). In any case, click on this backwards P and you will see all the punctuation in your text on the page. You'll see dots for spaces, etc. If you want to turn the visibility off, click the backwards P again. But you need it on for now. And, of course, this symbol shows up whenever you hit the enter key on the keyboard. If you have this button set to on, then you can see where your section breaks are, or whether you even have any. And like I said, you need to place one after every chapter. When I come to the end of a chapter, I will hit the return/enter key at least once. And then I'll add the section break. Here's how:

Go up to the blue ribbon and click on the **Layout** tab. Just below the word Layout, you will see the **Breaks** drop-down label. **Click on it** and then go down to the **Next Page** label. Click the **Next Page** label. At which point you should see the enter key symbol appear, followed by a line that is labelled Section Break (Next Page). This will appear in the exact spot you have your cursor, so make sure your cursor is where you want it (after the enter symbol at the end of the text of the chapter). And that's it. You want one of these **Section Breaks** after every chapter (or section). Later, when you are working with your headers and footers, if things aren't working out correctly, check to see if you are missing a section break. You may need to add one. Then if things are still screwy, it will have to do with the **link to previous** issue, more than likely.

This is important, so I'm going to repeat it:

IMPORTANT IMPORTANT   IMPORTANT

If you are having trouble with your headers (the title of the book on one page and your name on the other if you are writing a novel), or your footers (if you are putting your page numbers at the bottom of the page), the trouble will almost undoubtedly be due to one of two things:

1) **YOU NEED TO ADD A SECTION BREAK**.
or
2) **YOU NEED TO CLICK THE LINK TO PREVIOUS BUTTON to UNLINK PAGES/SECTIONS CLOSE BY WHERE THE PROBLEM IS LOCATED.**

I cannot stress the above problem/solution enough. I spent roughly three weeks to a month trying to figure out what the problem was and what to do about it. Finally, after searching for books about formatting in word, and watching YouTube video after YouTube video—Finally, someone pointed these two areas out in a video. So at least now I knew where to look. I still had to figure out exactly when to link or unlink. But at least I was headed in the right direction, now knowing the area to look in to solve the problem. I still struggled with all of it, for a time after that, trying to get things right. At this point I wanted to hunt down whoever came up with the Link to Previous button idea and strangle them. I had been ready to pull my hair out.

Okay, end of rant. So, let's continue. . .

If a Chapter Ends on an Odd Page:

Add a section break! Click on **Layout** (on blue ribbon), **Breaks**, then **Next Page** to add a section break at the end of the chapter. Then hit enter again, and add another section break (which will appear on the blank, even page). And this will move the cursor on to the next odd page where you can start the next chapter. Why? Because you're not supposed to have a chapter start on an even page. So basically, you will have clicked on Layout, Breaks, and Next Page, twice, with an extra tap of the enter key in between.

It is a weird thing, but open any book and you will see that the **odd** numbered pages are on the right-hand side. That's right! It doesn't seem natural, but that's the way it is. If you think about it, the chapter starting on an even page (the left-hand side) would mean that it is starting on the back of the previous page. There are books out there, that the author didn't adhere to this rule of thumb of starting chapters on the odd pages. I've seen it with short stories, too, which is probably less important than where a chapter starts. There will be the occasional book where one story ends and the next story begins, no matter what the page is that the previous story ended on. But, overall, most books adhere to this rule.

It has to do with the cover, sort of. If you open a book's cover, you'll see, the first page, technically (whether it is labelled as page one or not--which it usually isn't because the section you are looking at is front matter), is on the right-hand side. If you started on the left, the back of the cover would be page one.

That first page is usually the "Half-Title" page, in a paperback. This is followed by a full Title page, and the copyright page is on the back of this page; and then the other front matter follows . . . We'll cover all of this in a little bit.

***

Chapter Headings:

We've already touched on using the **Heading 1** button in the Styles section (On Home tab). **Right click** on it now and **select modify**. You will be able to see, and change, the Font and Font size here. If you want. Now look at the bottom of the dialog box. Do you see the **Format** button in the bottom left corner? Click on it and then move down and click on **Paragraph.** You'll see that this brings up the same dialog box we were in before (or a copy of it), when we were setting the line spacing. You could have gotten here by clicking in the Paragraph section, bottom right-hand corner arrow. Or by right-clicking and choosing paragraph. But we're here under the modify Header section. So, if we change anything, it will modify everything according to what we enter—and clicking on the Header button in the future, if we change anything now, it will be modified.

In any case, remember when I mentioned paying attention to the left side of the Spacing box? Look now at the Before and After. On my computer it is showing 12 for the number for *before*, and 0 for the number for *after*. You can change the Before figure, by increasing it (or decreasing it); but you want to increase this number in order to move the Chapter Heading down on the page, to try and get it to the center (or thereabouts). You can try these settings if you want: Set **Before** (using the dropdown arrows) to **162** and the **After** to **18** You can check the box for Auto Update and this should change all of your Headings for each chapter to this setting. You might have to play with this for each chapter and then go back and double check on previous and following chapters to see if they remain uniform. These settings, for some reason will, on occasion, shift as you work with the text, headings, etc. And often times you'll also see a space between the Headings listed beneath the Headings tab in the Navigation pane (remember, the window on the left-hand side of the screen, the Navigation pane, showing the tabs: Headings, Pages, and Results). You'll just have to kind of play around with this to try and keep it straight. But, like I said, the Chapter headings, followed by the chapter text, should start halfway down on the odd page (right hand page) where the chapter starts. You can click on Pages heading in the Navigation pane and use the side bar to scroll down to check that first pages are all showing print halfway down on the page for each chapter.

***

Headers and Footers:

To Bring up Header and Footer Tools:
Go to, or place cursor in, the **Top Margin** or the **Bottom Margin** of your manuscript and **double click** to bring up **Header and Footer Tools** Menu on ribbon. This menu will pop up between the Help and the Lightbulb. After this menu appears, just below where it says Header & Footer Tools, you will see another tab (highlighted with a white

background against the blue ribbon—you can't miss it) that reads Header & Footer. Directly below the Header & Footer label you will see three checkboxes with labels:

Different First Page
Different Odd & Even Pages
Show Document Text

Immediately to the left of this is the dreaded **Link to Previous** button. This button will either be highlighted or not. If this button is highlighted, then the right-hand sign/tab on the line indicating header/footer area in the margin of your manuscript will read **Same as Previous**.

At the top of your screen, just below the blue ribbon, if you look to the far left, you will see a Header & Footer section. Within this section you will see **Header**, **Footer**, and **Page #** icons.

To close out of the Header/Footer section just click on the white X in the red box on the far right. Or you can simply move down to the body of your text (anywhere on the page that isn't the margin area) and double click.

Okay, so here comes the crazy section. Open a book, a novel, and look at the top of the page, above the text. You'll probably see the book title on one side and the author's name on the other. The author's name is usually on the left side/Even pages, and the book title is usually on the right side/Odd pages. Sometimes the words (of headers) are in all caps, and sometimes just the first letter is capitalized. It varies. And, in books of short stories, sometimes (probably most times) the title of whatever story the book is open to will be displayed at the top of the page. This is how I did my first short story collection, and most of the ones that followed. I had to "unlink" the pages, or sections where the story changed names. When the book is a novel, you only have to deal with this once. You set up the header for the odd pages (Book title) and the header for the even pages (Your name). Once you set it up, you are good to go. The only problem then is removing the headings/page numbers from the blank pages, and the first page of each Chapter (which means unlinking).

You can set up the page numbers to display at the top of the page, or at the bottom. I usually set them on the bottom.

Okay, so here goes . . .

How do you get to the Header and footer controls? Okay, we just did it a minute ago.

Well, when you have text, and a good bit of it, say two or three chapters, you can just go to the very top section of the page, the margin area, and double click the left mouse button. You might have to give it a couple of tries to get it to pop up. But once you get it to display, you'll know it. There will be a line at the bottom of the margin and it will have a little sign on each side of the page, right there on the line. The left side sign will read: **Odd Page Header** (if you are on an odd page, and at the top of the page), and this will be followed by a dash and then something like **Section 8** (or whatever section you are in—remember the section breaks?). If you look at the bottom of the page, the same message will be displayed, only it will say **Odd Page Footer-Section 8** on the left side to indicate footer as opposed to header.

On the right-hand side of each line, both top and bottom, you will see the **Same as Previous** label.

If you click in the upper margin, or the lower margin areas, thus bringing up the Header & Footer menu at the top of the screen—The **Link to**

Previous button will either be highlighted or not. If this button is highlighted, then the right-hand sign/tab on the line indicating header/footer area (in page margin) will read **Same as Previous**. If the cursor is in the top margin, or Header area, and you click on the **Highlighted Link to Previous** button, the little sign reading Same as Previous will disappear. If this sign is gone, then the page header is "unlinked" from the previous page, or section, and the Link to Previous button is no longer highlighted. Same thing for footer if the cursor is in the bottom margin, or footer section. If "unlinked" the sign is gone.

If you click on the **Link to Previous** button again, a dialog box will pop up, asking if you want to "delete this Header/Footer and connect to the previous Header/Footer in the previous section?" Basically, it is just asking if you want to re-connect. If you click *yes*, you will notice the **Same as Previous label** will reappear in the header/footer section of the page you are on.

All of this is rather confusing, I know. You just have to work with it and get used to it. It will still drive you crazy though, trust me. *It is always better to lean towards unlinking things if you are having problems.* I'll come back to all of this in a second. But first, let's

Add a Header:

The brief version:

Double-click in upper margin of page in your manuscript.
Click on **Header** icon (first icon under blue ribbon on left-hand side, just under File)
Click on **Blank** (first item in list)
Replace the [Type Here] which will appear in upper margin by highlighting and typing.
Center the header by clicking Home on ribbon and clicking on second icon in paragraph section.

The detailed walkthrough:

To add a Header to your book, double click in the margin area at the top of the page, just like we have done. Okay. Now the Header & Footer Menu is active.

Go to the far left of the menu/section, just below the blue ribbon.

Click on the **Header** icon (just below File on the blue ribbon).

The very first item that displays will read Blank. When you hover the cursor over the box (where it reads *Type Here* in brackets) it will read Blank and Blank Header. Click in the box to activate it. The [Type Here] will appear at the top of the page of whatever page you are on. You replace this text with either your name (if you are on an even page) or the book title (if you are on an odd page). The way I always remember which is on which page is that I imagine someone looking at a book and they exclaim, "This is an ODD title for a book!" Anyway, it works for me. You don't want them saying your name is odd; that would be rude. So, of course, they only say that about the title. So, the title is on the odd page, and your name is on the even page (as a general rule).

Once you type out the Header, you can go to home page to click on second icon in the bottom of the paragraph section to center whatever you just typed. If the **Different Odd and Even Pages** box is checked (on the Header & Footer menu—remember, just to the right of the Link to Previous button) then the Header that you just typed will appear on all Odd pages, or all Even pages, depending on whether your cursor was on an odd or an even page when you typed the Header. Then you do the same thing you just did, for the opposite page. Place the cursor on the Header section at the top of the page (odd or even, whichever has no heading). Then go to far left and Click on the Header icon (below File) and click on Blank box (first one at top of list). The message telling you to [Type Here] will appear at the top of the page. Type whichever (Your name or book title), and then center it. This will appear on all odd or all even pages (again, depending on which page (even or odd) you are working on.) if the checkbox is checked for Different Odd and Even Pages. And whether the pages are linked (Link to Previous button selected) will determine if the heading appears on all of the following pages.

To Add Page Numbers:

Go to bottom of page, to the margin area, and double click to bring up footer box (if the menu is not still displayed) and then go up to Header & Footer menu once it is activated.

On far left, below the blue ribbon, you will see the third icon in from left, which is the **Page Number icon**. **Click on this**, then go down the list and **Click** on where it reads **Bottom of Page** and then **Click** on **Plain Number 2**. And your page numbers will appear on all the pages. Just like magic!

And now comes the tricky part: Removing Headers and Page numbers from blank pages and from first pages of chapters. And why must you remove these headers and page numbers that you've just added? Because, remember, you shouldn't have headers and page numbers on blank pages, or on pages where the chapter begins.

Removing Headers and Page Numbers:

Okay, first go to a page where you have the beginning of a Chapter. Once you are on that page, click on upper margin area of your manuscript to bring up the Header/Footer menu. Click on the **Link to Previous** button if it is highlighted. You'll see that the **Same as Previous** sign has disappeared from the line below header, indicating that the header on this page is unlinked from previous page. Do the same thing you just did for the header section again—only this time, do it in the footer section by clicking in the footer area to bring curser there and then going up to top and clicking on the **Link to Previous** button. Again, this unlinks the bottom or footer.

Now go back up and check the box that says different first page, if it isn't checked. Sometimes you'll have to click the **Link to Previous** button again, if it returns to being highlighted. There is an order to this. If you tick the **Different first page** box before clicking the **Link to Previous button**, I believe you'll be okay. I often get the order confused.

In any case, the header for that page should have disappeared. And the page number should also be gone. If the page number is not gone, it will often be highlighted. In which case you just hit the delete key. Sometimes you have to hit the delete key twice to get the number to actually disappear.

Complications:
If Page Number disappears

And here is something strange that often happens on the next page (the page just behind the one the Chapter started on). When you remove the header and page number on the chapter start page, the number on the next page disappears also. If this happens, place your cursor at the bottom section of the second page (the page after the chapter-start page), and double click to bring up the Header/Footer menu (if it isn't already up). Now go up to the **Page #** icon at top of screen (on left below blue ribbon, the third icon from left). **Click** on **Page #** icon. **Hover** over **Bottom of page** and then click on **Plain Number 2**. Okay, I always put my page number on bottom of page. You might decide that you want your page number at top of page. That is fine. I imagine it all works basically the same. You'll just have to figure out the adjustments you need to make. I'm simply giving you instructions for how I do it. After you've clicked on the Plain Number 2, your page number should then properly reappear. If the number does not reappear, or if it is incorrect, then go through the process of unlinking the page from the previous page. By clicking in upper margin section and clicking on highlighted **Link to Previous** button, and then doing the same for the bottom/footer section. Just like we did earlier. You'll find yourself continually jumping back and forth between clicking the **Link to Previous** button to unlink, and the **Page#** icon to hover and then click on **Plain Number 2.** Trust me, you are going to spend a lot of time fooling around with the header/footer section and the page number section. At least until you get a handle on it all. There is another section under the Page# menu: **Format page numbers**.

Before we move on to formatting the page numbers, you might want to go ahead and remove the headers and footers from the blank pages you have in the manuscript. You know, when your chapter ended on an odd page and you had to hit the section break twice to move on to the next odd page for the beginning of the following chapter. Yep, those are the ones. And so all you do is the same thing you have done to remove the headers and page numbers so far. First, of course, unlink that page from the other pages by clicking the **Link to Previous** button to make the **Same as Previous** tags/signs disappear. If you delete a header and/or footer and the rest of the headers/footers disappear from any or all of the pages before and/or after the page you are actually working on; Well, that means you need to unlink that page. Or you might be missing a section break somewhere . . . You'll just have to keep checking these two things. Check to make sure the backward P is clicked on so you can see the punctuation and where your section breaks are. It is almost a straight-up guarantee one of these two things IS the problem: You don't have a section break, or you need to UNLINK the Link to Previous.

Front matter and formatting page numbers:

Okay, so you maybe have a blank page on the screen; The beginning of a whole new document. This would be one that you intend on copying and pasting the text of your novel into. Or maybe you just add blank pages to the front of your novel file. There are several ways to do this, but since I usually have to copy and paste in my stories to make up my book anyway, I'll usually start fresh. I open a blank document and move down the page and type Title, or My Title. I highlight it and then increase the font size. I make sure the title is in the middle of the page. Then place the cursor at the end of this and hit the enter key. This will be my half title page. I then **add a section break** to move on to the next page. And, of course, I have to **add a second section break** to move to what will be the next odd page. I copy and paste my title again, about halfway down the page and add my byline (my author name). And perhaps I add a subtitle just beneath the title, etc. This page will be my full title page. So, then I add another section break and move to the next page. This time I only have one section break, because the copyright page is the one that comes next, and it is usually always on the back of the title page (don't know why). So I type the word Copyright, just so I know.

Just a small note here:
When you type out your copyright information for real--And you can do that now if you want—In case you were wondering how to get that famous Copyright Symbol ©

Just **hold down the alt key** and **type 0169** on your keypad.

After I've set up the copyright page; then, I add a section break and move on to the next page (which should be an odd page already). And on this new odd page I type dedication just in case I want to put one in my book. Then I add two section breaks to move on to the next odd page. Of course, I'm going to need a page for the table of contents, so that will be my next odd page (after I add the two section breaks).
In all, I usually end up adding at least six pages. Sometimes two more than this, just in case I want to add an introduction--or for a prelude, etc. In any

case, I've got a series of pages, an even number of them.

Then I go through and unlink them all. Each and every one of the pages. I go to top and bottom of pages and click on the Link to Previous button for all of them, twice for each page (once at top and once at bottom), just to remove the Same as Previous signs. Okay, after all of this I'm safe. No headaches (in theory).

Okay, then I move to the next odd page. I should already be there if I've added a section break to the last even page.

I copy in the first chapter of my novel/book here. I go to the end of the text of the first chapter and add a section break. And if that chapter ends on an odd page, what do I do? You got it! I add the second section break. Then I copy and paste in chapter two and add another section break at the end of chapter two. And then I bring in my third chapter and do the same.

So I've got three chapters. Here's what I do: I go back to chapter one and unlink it. I make sure the checkbox is checked for **different first page**. I could have already set up my headers prior to this. I don't think that the order matters. If I have set up the headers, then the header will disappear when I check the different first page box. I then go to bottom of the page (where chapter one starts). I then go up to **Page #** icon click it and then down to **Format Page Numbers.** I click this and a box with the labelled Page Number Format pops up. Here I go down to the radio buttons and make sure I click on the one that says **Start at**. When I change the button to Start at, a number one will appear in the box automatically. I hit ok (If this *is* chapter one, or Prelude, which means I want the number one) to close out the dialog box. If a number appears at the bottom of this page, then it should be a number 1. The page will really be a page 7 or page 9 or whatever (remember the front matter still counts in total page count), which will show in the total number count at the bottom of the screen on the left, right next to the word count. If the number does appear at the bottom of the page, I highlight (it is probably already highlighted) and delete it. Why? Because this is the first page of a chapter (no Headings or page numbers).

Then I go to the next page to see if the number has changed to number two. Or perhaps it has disappeared. And if it *has* disappeared, what do I do? I, of course, go up and click on the **Page #** icon and then down to where it says **Bottom of Page**, and when the menu rolls out, I click on **Plain Number 2**. If everything appears in order now, with all of the page numbers correct and what not, and the headers (if I've added them prior to this) are all okay, well, then I go back to the front matter.

In the front matter section, I won't have many page numbers. And if I do, I'll probably make them Roman numerals (as I mentioned earlier). When we were on the format page number dialog box and changed the radio button from **Continue from** to **Start at**. Well, at the top of that box is a drop-down arrow box to change the numbers to Roman numeral. Let's go back and take a look. Do you remember how we got there? Right, we double-clicked in the margin (top or bottom) to bring up the header/footer menu, then went over and clicked on the **Page #** icon. Then we went down and clicked on **Format Page Numbers.** That brings the dialog box right up, and there it is, right at the top: **Number Format.** Voila! We just use the little drop arrow to find the **iii**, or whatever and we've got our numbers changed to Roman numerals. We will have to individually work with each page, since we have them unlinked, hopefully. And we might have to go back to the Format Page Number dialog and change the radio button Continue from . . . or whatever.

In any case, we go through and make sure that everything is ok. We, of course, make sure the page numbering is correct and that there are no headers and page numbers on the blank pages. Or on the first page of every chapter in the main section of the manuscript. Of course, we, if that is all we brought in, only have three chapters to work with. The main thing here is to make sure that the page numbers are running in order, and that the headers are all correct, with the name of the book on the odd pages and the author name on the even pages. We make sure that there are no pages without headers or page numbers if the pages have text on them (except in the front matter section). If there is a page without a header, or page number, then we have to solve the problem. We'll have to see if there is a section break, or if the page needs to be linked or unlinked, etc. And if a number is missing then we go and click the plain number two. We might have to play around a bit to get things organized. And we should have our margins and fonts set up exactly how we want them. And the line spacing.

And now we bring in the rest of our chapters, the rest of the book. Once we bring it all into the document, everything should match up fine. All of the headers should roll out onto the added pages perfectly; and the page numbers should do the same. Often times, I'll format the story (if that's what I've got) to the proper settings before bringing it into the main manuscript, and then check it again by selecting that story/chapter to make sure it matches all the numbers. And of course, for each first chapter page we have to go through and delete the headers and page numbers.

And we're probably editing the text where errors pop up or new wording hits us, new ideas, etc. And this might cause a story/chapter to end on a new page, odd or even, and throw things off. If this happens, we might have to go in and delete a section break, or add a new one.

And finally, when we finish all of this, we need to add a table of contents.

Adding a table of contents:

Scroll up to the blank page in the front matter where you want to place the table of contents and click to place cursor. Then go to top of screen. Click on **References** tab (on blue ribbon, just to the right of Layout)

Click on the **Table of Contents** tab (very first one on left, right under File on ribbon
Pick whichever style of TOC you want from dropdown list by clicking on it.

Before you add the table of contents, you need to go through and select your chapter headings (highlighting them with cursor) and then click on **Heading 1** button in the **Styles menu** (on Home tab, fourth section over from left, beneath blue ribbon). You need to do this for each chapter heading you want listed in the table of contents. You will especially need to do this if your book is a collection of short stories. Select each title.

If you have your Navigation pane open (on left of your screen with headings: Headings, Pages, Results), and have Headings selected, then each time you select a title and click on the heading 1 button, you will see that heading/chapter title (or story title) appear in the Headings list. This is generally what gets pulled into the table of contents when TOC is created.

When the TOC (Table of Contents) appears on blank page that you selected, you will see that TOC lists the page numbers for each chapter/story title/heading.

Each one of the Headings (chapter title/story title) listed should be followed by an odd page number (at least for fiction). If not, then something is out of whack. Perhaps you have edited a story/chapter, and the text ran over, pushing onto an odd page; And this might have pushed the beginning of the next chapter onto an even page. Fear not.

Just click on the Heading (in the TOC or in the Navigation Pane) that is on the even page, and that page will be displayed. You can then scroll up to the end of the previous chapter and insert a section break by clicking on Layout, then Breaks, then Next Page. This should push the chapter that is beginning on an even page over to the proper Odd page, where it should properly begin. Of course, you might then have an extra blank page that you need to go and delete out (by deleting the section break, which can sometimes be tricky).

You can also scroll through the pages if you have the **Pages** heading of the Navigation pane (if Navigation pane isn't showing, go to/Click on **View** on Ribbon at top and check the Navigation pane box in *Show* section) selected instead of Headings, and look for the chapter start pages (The pages with the blank space showing at the top of the page/Title or chapter heading showing). And beneath these pages, the page number is listed. You can click on whatever page you need to click on here, to jump directly to the page you need. This is all pretty intuitive. I'm just mentioning it.

Okay, after you have made your corrections, and added the section break or whatever, to push the chapter start to the odd page. You will need to update the TOC, because it will still be listing the page number that the chapter start was on before you corrected things. It is always good to recheck the TOC after you make any changes to your manuscript, just to make sure everything is correct and matches up.

So, update the table now by

Clicking on the References tab

Then click on **Update Table** icon (just to the right of the TOC icon (which is on the far left on the bar beneath the blue ribbon)). If the Update Table button is grayed out, you'll probably need to click on your TOC page. Once you do this, the Update Table button should be highlighted.

Once you click on the **Update Table** icon, you will get a dialog box asking whether you just want to update page numbers or the whole table. Most of the time you will just need to update the page numbers.

Now read them over to make sure all of the page numbers in the table of contents are odd pages and match the proper start of the chapters/stories.

Of course, there could be the case that you don't need or want a TOC. Or, that you have some reason for not wanting everything on odd pages.
For example, if the copyright page is listed in the TOC, then it will be listed as being on an even page, because it is, in fact, on an even page (the back of your title page, which is exactly where it should be)
But, do you want the copyright page listed in the TOC at all? You'll have to decide. The best thing to do is look in the front of published books that are similar to yours to find answers to most of your questions regarding front matter, what's listed in TOC, etc. You might even have questions regarding what comes before the TOC and exactly what comes after . . .

*And remember when I mentioned everything working out just fine (In theory)? For the most part it will, but . . .

I want to warn you though, that often times, even when you have everything correct, things can get *screwy. As an example, I was just working on for-matting for one of my fiction books, as I'm writing this. I've been jumping back and forth, clicking buttons to format things properly in one manuscript and then jumping to this one to write down what exactly I did. I had everything pretty much format-ted in the book and then decided to change things. I copied and pasted a blurb that I wanted in the front of the book. I simply moved it to the odd page that would be in front of the Table of Contents page (The contents page would start on the next odd page, of course). Well, suddenly, for some inexpli-cable reason, page number 1 (which had been the start of the first chapter/story – even though it wasn't visible on that page) jumped to the TOC page. I made sure I had everything unlinked, etc. and then checked the **different first page** check box. And then I fooled with the page # section, all of it. No luck. I still don't know why this happened. Perhaps the easiest thing would have been to simply delete the TOC and start over. Instead, I added two more section breaks, more pages, etc. Then unlinked those pages. Changed page numbers then and finally got the front matter separated from the rest once again. And then I deleted the ex-tra pages, by deleting the breaks. I still can't* *explain what happened. The main thing to remember is that when things get screwy, you will at least know which buttons to start working with to fix the problem—then you get creative from there.*

I know that all of this can seem very confusing. I apologize. But it just seems confusing reading it. If you actually go and look for the buttons, etc. then it will become easier as you work through it. If you feel completely overwhelmed, take a break. Walk away for a few minutes. Don't give up. It all can easily become overwhelming. Like I said, it took me three weeks to format my first manuscript. I'm trying to make it so you will not have to go through that. There will come a time when you can do this in a couple of hours (and everything will fall into place like clockwork). Some people might do it in even less time. I take my time, however. If you are speedy, and things fall right into place, hey, I applaud you!

Cleaning up your text:

These are not big issues.

Hyphenation

I don't know whether you noticed it or not, but the hyphenation button is under the **Layout** menu. Perhaps you want to automatically hyphenate your text to tidy things up a bit. If this is something you want (I usually use it), just click on the hyphenation button and in the drop-down menu you can change the **None** option to **Automatic** or **Manual**.

I have had some issues, however, where I have used the automatic hyphenation and then changed something in the manuscript and the word is then moved to the middle of the page or whatever and still has the hyphenation (the "-") showing. Just keep an eye out.

Drop Caps

Note: You'll need to do this later (if you want drop caps) after you create your ebook.

What Drop Caps are (and you probably already know this):

You know, when the start of the first line of the first paragraph of a Chapter has the large letter to make things look a little more fancy. Some people use them, some don't. Some people make the whole first sentence larger in font size. There are any number of things you can do.

To create/apply drop caps:

Place the cursor next to (on the left side of) the first line of text (of the first paragraph of chapter) and delete any indentation you might have by hitting the backspace key. Bring the line all the way over to the edge of the margin.

Then, to add the drop cap, go to the **Insert** tab on the blue ribbon (just to the right of the Home tab) and look all the way over toward the right-hand side of the screen on the bar just below the blue ribbon. You will see the **text** section. Just to the right of a crooked letter 'A' there is an icon with a large A with lines beside and below it on the icon. Below this are the words **Drop Cap** and a small arrow pointing down. **Click on this** and you will see a list that says None, Dropped, etc. If you have your cursor at the first line of text, when you hover over the word

Dropped in the menu, you'll see the first letter become larger and extend down three lines or so, pushing text over. You can click on this to keep it. I usually do use drop caps, but **Not Yet!** Don't do anything too fancy yet . . .

Copyright Symbol ©

I've mentioned this elsewhere, but wanted to have
this info conveniently accessible from the head-
ings/TOC of this book. So here it is again. How to
get the copyright symbol: **alt+0169**
Hold down the alt key and type 0169 on numeric
key pad.

Check everything over, making sure all is in order.

Checklist:

1) Trim size correct
2) Margins correct
3) Font style and Font size correct
4) All chapters starting on odd pages
5) No page numbers or headers on the chapter start pages
6) No page numbers or headers on blank pages.
7) Is Front matter set up how you want it? Half Title, Title, copyright, etc.
8) Back matter (acknowledgements, etc.) should also be checked if you have any.
9) Does manuscript end on an even page?

First, look back over the manuscript you have here and make sure everything is exactly how you want it. Is everything nice and neat? Have you got all of your chapters starting on odd pages? Are all of your blank pages free of headers and page numbers? Be sure and double check that the beginning pages of each chapter are free of headers and page numbers also. And, check that the chapter titles start halfway down the page. Check the **before** number for each chapter beginning (which is what pushes the text down the page when you increase it. Remember, it is in the line spacing box) to make sure the number matches for each chapter beginning. Check to make sure your font style and font size are what you want (I generally use Georgia). Check to make sure you've got the margins, trim size, and everything set like you want it. Simply put, check over everything.

Make a Copy of your now-perfect manuscript

We have come to the fork in the road. You are working on an **ebook** and a **paperback book**, correct? You can use this file as your main file and can either make two copies or just keep one and do the ebook first. If you decide to make two copies: Create one copy to use for ebook, and then another copy to use, or work with as your paperback. and then add the bells and whistles (Drop caps, fancy first lines, etc.) to the paperback copy (whether it is this file, or a new copy) and then set this **paperback** file aside.

You will have two different files to upload. You are going to create the **ebook file** and then also the **paperback file** for uploading:

If you know what to do with your word file from here then fine. You can go ahead and add the drop caps and whatever else you want to do. Essentially, you are finished with the formatting side of things. You can skip the rest of this book, or at least the next two sections.
If you don't know what to do yet, or how to prepare your manuscript for publication, then . . .

To Prepare/Publish your ebook:

Here is what you do . . .

Download Kindle Create (if you haven't already done so)

Eeek! What? Really?

I know. I hear you groaning. Everybody hates it. I understand. I just use it for uploading purposes.

Here is my reasoning:

If you want the upload to Amazon to be super easy (and I do), then use their software. It is as simple as that!

I've got this analogy:

Perhaps I had the title to the book Save the Cat in mind (it is on my *to read* list), but I'm thinking that uploading any other file (at least as far as the ebook goes) is like standing before an elevator holding a cat (your manuscript file). You push the up button (to upload) and the elevator doors open. You reach in and hit the button for the roof, or the top floor (wherever you imagine Amazon to be). Personally, I imagine a helicopter waiting on the roof to transport my file to Amazon. So, you are holding the cat and it is squirming. You hit the proper button and wait on the elevator doors to almost close. You want just enough of an opening to toss the cat in before the doors close completely. Then you stand there and heave a sigh of relief. However, you *do* cross your fingers and hope for the best. You hope that everything is going to work out fine on the other end. You, if you are like me, imagine that Amazon employee waiting on the elevator door to open and your manuscript file (the cat) to be there. Now, that employee is supposed to catch the cat and take it over to the waiting helicopter which will whisk your manuscript(cat) away to Amazon . . .

And what sort of condition, or state, do you think that feline is going to be in when those elevator doors open? Hmm?

I see the Kindle Create software as a humane little container that was built by Amazon to transport manuscripts/cats. You, of course, gently place your cooperative little feline in this box and shut the tiny door. The Amazon employee has no problem on the other end. He or she is very familiar with these boxes and what is inside. The Amazon employee simply picks up the box and walks it calmly to the waiting helicopter. End of story—well, not exactly.

Your story/book will be easily published and spread to the world . . . End of analogy.

It might be better to think of it like when you are going through the drive-through at the bank. You put your check, license, etc. in the tube and it swooshes right up. Just think of the bank as Amazon KDP, and Kindle Create as the tube—you stick your manuscript into it and Swoosh! No problemo!

Am I saying for you to use Kindle Create to write/create your masterpiece? Absolutely not! The software is not really up to par for that. One day it might be, who knows?

But today, NO! The software is extremely limited. However, it is the perfect vehicle for uploading your manuscript with ease. It is Amazon's software. How can the upload fail?

Initially, when I was first trying to figure things out, I tried using other forms of whatever type file . . . but it was a headache. I tried Scrivener, which is a superb writing/outlining tool. And you can compile into many different formats, which is fantastic. Somehow, I couldn't get the Kindle Gen software that I had to download to use in conjunction with Scrivener to play nice. There were issues. I tried a few other things. Nothing seemed to work great. It was as though they didn't even want my creative masterpiece! Hee hee.

So, I ended up trying out the Kindle Create software. I even wrote a small book in the software while learning to use it. The trouble is, it is next to impossible, if not *totally* impossible to get my work out of Kindle Create. I've been told that it can't be done. I'm going to try a few things one day and see. It was a good book, written under a pseudonym, just to try things out. But I knew I probably wasn't going to publish it in paperback. So be it.

Okay, so there is NOT a whole lot you have to do to import your word file manuscript into the kindle create software. You will need to do a few things, however, make adjustments, etc., once you get the manuscript into the kindle create software.

So, **download Kindle Create** (from the KDP/Amazon site) if you haven't done so.

Open Kindle Create
You will see **Create New** button Click it.

If you have used an older version of Kindle Create, or already have KC, and have other KC files on your computer, you will see **Open Existing File** also listed.

You can look over the File Edit View and Help menus at the top of the box if you so choose.

On the left-hand side of the window, in descending order, you will see listed: **REFLOWABLE**, **COMICS**, and **PRINT REPLICA**.

Click on, or Highlight **REFLOWABLE**
Look in the lower right-hand corner of the window.

Click on **Choose File (.doc, .docx)**

A box will pop up for you to browse to locate the proper manuscript file on your computer. Do this now. Find the Word document and then
Click **Open**
You will see a message that reads something like
Importing and converting your document.
There will be a lot of activity at this point. Just wait until you see "Import Successful."
Click the **Continue** button

Click the **Get Started** button

You will then see a list of items with checkboxes beside them. These are a list of headings that will appear in your book's table of contents.

Uncheck whichever boxes you don't need, or don't want. If you have both a Half title page, and a Full title page, both of these will be checked. You could have left the Half title page out, or deleted it before opening the document in the kindle create software, as you really don't need both in the ebook (in my opinion). Uncheck the Half title page along with whatever else you don't want showing in the TOC.

Click **Accept Selected**

Voila! Your book is in kindle create.

You will notice that there is a clickable **Table of Contents.**

*** An Important Note Here:

In earlier versions of Kindle Create, you would bring your whole document into KC (just as I've had you do). However, in this newest version of KC you can remove all of the front matter (title pages, copyright page, dedication, etc.) and any backmatter (acknowledgements, etc.) you might have. It used to be that you would simply locate the cursor on your Title, and then click on **Title** listed in the **elements** section on the right-hand side of the screen. Now, this has moved to the left. You will see there are bars listed on the left-hand side of KC that read **Front Matter**, **Body**, and **Back Matter**. If you don't see the Back Matter bar, just click anywhere on the Body bar (except on the plus sign) and the Back Matter bar will appear. Or you can scroll down using the side scroller.

Now, with this newer version of KC, you simply click on the Plus Sign on **Front Matter** bar and fill in the boxes that appear when you click on one of the items that appear on the list. For instance, if you click on Title in the list, a box opens with a form for you to fill in with the corresponding information.

Personally, I prefer the old way, but that's just me.

So, at this point have three choices:

You can delete out all of the front matter info that you just brought into KC when you brought in your full manuscript, and then click on the plus sign and fill in the forms.

Or you can redo the setup process by deleting the front matter before pulling in just the body of your manuscript.

Or you can leave things as they are. Up to you.

Now, if you look at the Navigation pane on the left-hand side of the screen (if you don't see it, click on the Body bar again and it should reappear). In this pane you will see a list of all of your Chapter titles (or story titles). You will probably see other headings listed. Everything listed should be from the checked boxes when you first brought in the manuscript.

You will also see large orange dots next to a few of the items. Sometimes these dots will appear beside something that was supposed to be a Chapter Title, but it just didn't get picked up as such. It happens sometimes. Here's what you do to fix things:

In the Navigation pane, click on the Chapter Title with the orange dot beside it (the Chapter Title that didn't get picked up). When you click on this heading, you should see the manuscript shift to the page with that heading. The cursor will already be in place on the header for the chapter. Now look at the right-hand pane of KC screen. You should see two labels listed side by side a short distance down the pane: **Elements**, and **Formatting**. Click on the Elements label. Below this, you should see a label for **Chapter Title**. Click on it. Now, if you look back at the left-hand Navigation pane, you will see that the orange dot has disappeared and the chapter heading looks like the other headings in the list. Do this for any other Chapter Title that didn't properly get picked up.

You can either click on the headings in the Navigation pane to maneuver around your document, or you can Go to the table of contents page and click on the various titles of chapters, or short stories, if that is what you have. You can easily jump to whichever chapter/story you desire.

Of course, if you have deleted out the TOC when you deleted out the rest of the front matter, you'll have to add a new one. You can insert TOC by going to the Front Matter bar, and clicking on the plus sign, or by going to the **Insert** label at the top left of the screen and clicking to find TOC in the list.

If you wait a few minutes, you'll see a bar with an orange triangle and a message that says something like *You haven't saved in a while would you like to save now?* Just hit enter, or

Click the **Save** button, which is located in the upper right corner of the window.

The first time you save, you have the option of saving under whatever name you want to save the file as, much like in Microsoft Word and other programs. Pretty standard.

Overall, the KC software is pretty intuitive. There aren't a lot of bells and whistles, but they add a little more with each update.

And, of course, there are some glitches.

In this new version, I've noticed that if you use the **Find** feature at the top of the screen to search out specific words, etc. the find dialog box doesn't have a cancel button, or an X for closing out the box. I had to hit the Undo arrow (which was grayed out) to make it disappear; whereupon it just went to the taskbar on my computer and it had an X showing there to close the box. I then discovered that the ESC key on the keyboard works. Why didn't I think of that initially?

So anyway . . .

Scroll through your document now and notice how nice and clean everything looks. All that time you spent formatting and then tidying up your manuscript paid off.

As you are scrolling through the book, however, you might notice that there are no headers or page numbers in your ebook document. Was all of that work—all the struggling with the Link to Previous button, etc.—necessary? Did you just waste all that time for nothing?

It *was* necessary! You didn't waste your time; You will need the headers and page numbers, of course, for the paperback version of your book. Also, ebooks don't necessarily use page numbers. They are set up to use location numbers, or percentage of the book read, etc. The reason for this, I'm guessing, is due to the fact that for ebooks the size of the font can be changed by each reader. Not to mention the fact that also, the text shows up different on different devices. All you are concerned with is how neat it looks on each of the different devices. And you want your book to look perfect on all devices, of course.

Okay, so once you have scrolled through your book and seen how nice it looks, you can take it all a step further and use the **Preview** feature at the top right of the window (right next to the **Save** icon). Play around with the features now if you want and see how things will look on a tablet, etc. Use the arrow buttons to move through the document. Change the font size, etc. Just experiment and check it out. When you are finished, close out the Previewer and you will be back in the KC main window.

Now, remember the Elements and Formatting labels in the top section of the right-hand pane in Kindle Create? Find them now. You will see that the right-hand label, just next to the Elements label, reads **Formatting.** Of course it does, nothing has changed from when you used the Elements tab earlier.

If you click on this Formatting tab, you'll see a list of editing tools/functions. This list isn't too extensive, but you can do some basic formatting. For instance, remember when we held off doing Drop Caps in Word? Well, you will note that Drop Caps is in this editing tool list.

Let's do the drop caps now. There are two ways to do this:

Go to the first page of the first chapter of your manuscript and put/click the cursor right next to the first line of text, right at the beginning of the first paragraph. Be sure that there are no indentations. If there are any indentations, delete them. You won't be able to do this the normal way (using the backspace key like in Word). You will probably have to do get rid of the indented space by dropping down (in the right-hand panel of KC) to the **Indents** tab, which is just below Drop Caps. Go to the second icon down. Use the arrows to the right (the bottom arrow) to change the indentation to zero. You'll see your text move as you do this. Again, this is the second icon down. Bring the text right up to the margin.

Once the text is right at the margin, and your cursor is in place, go back up (still in the right-hand pane) and click on the check box beside **Apply Drop Cap** to apply it.

If you want to use drop caps that is all you do. You just need to go through and do this for each and every chapter. If your chapter starts with dialogue, then you might want to highlight the quote marks and the first letter. And sometimes this looks awful. You can use them or not, up to you!

And the Second Way to **apply drop caps**:

You don't even have to have your cursor clicked at the beginning of the first paragraph. You can have the cursor anywhere on the first page. With this method you don't have to worry if the text is indented.

In the right-hand navigation pane, if you are still on **Formatting** switch and Click on the **Elements** tab. **Click** on the third tab down, which says **Chapter First Paragraph**. Voila! Drop Cap will be immediately applied. If you click on the **Chapter First Paragraph** and nothing happens, look up at the top of the panel to where it says Current Element. If it says Chapter First Paragraph beneath this, click on **Clear** button to the right and the heading should switch to

Body Text. Then go back and click on the Chapter First Paragraph button again. It should work this time. Granted, this second way can seem a little more involved if you aren't exactly where you need to be and things aren't just right. So you might just stick to the first way. Just letting you know there are options.

IMPORTANT: There is a reason that we didn't apply the drop caps to the Word file before bringing the file into Kindle Create. Often times, the drop caps get screwy in the transition. If you ever open an ebook on kindle and see a huge letter at the top of the line of text, well that is what happened. The huge letter will be sitting just above the text instead of in its proper place. I've had this happen when I tried to upload my doc/docx file straight to the ebook upload tab on Amazon (If I am remembering correctly, or perhaps it was a pdf file--Whatever the other option(s) is(are)). I published my book and downloaded it, only to see the drop cap letter sitting above the first line of text. That is one of the reasons why I use Kindle Create. Once you pull the file into KC (Kindle Create) and make the minor adjustments, what you see in the previewer is pretty much exactly the way your masterpiece is going to look on the kindle or the reader software on your tablet . . . The only exception being that once you are reading, changing fonts of reader, etc. It might look different then.

Drop caps can get screwy no matter the program. I've used Calibre software and played around. For whatever reason, the drop caps get to looking screwy if you put them into the MS Word document and then use a converter program such as Calibre to convert the Word doc/docx (actually, I believe Calibre only accepts one of these, **doc** or **docx**, not both) file to epub or mobi, etc. Sometimes the drop caps will look passable, but not great. And then if you want to correct things, you have to work with the html file (in Calibre). In any case, you won't have to worry about all of that for Amazon—if you use KC.

I will also mention that in this newest version of KC, when I forgot to remove drop caps from my Word doc before bringing it into KC, the transfer didn't seem bad. I only had a chapter or two where the drop cap shifted. It wasn't totally out of whack like would happen with previous versions of the software. It wasn't sitting on top of the body of text like used to happen. Maybe they got the glitch worked out.

Of course, using drop caps is optional. You might not want to use them, like I said. Or you could decide, instead, to simply make the first three or four words of the beginning paragraph of each chapter a little larger font, or perhaps make the first few words bold. You can do all of this in KC easily enough:

In the right-hand pane, switch from the Elements setting at the top to Formatting. Highlight with the cursor the text you want to change, whether it be the first three or four words of the first line of the first paragraph, or whatever you decide and click the B for bold, or use the dropdown arrow to change the font to a larger size. If these buttons are grayed out and seemingly inaccessible, it is only because you haven't clicked or highlighted any text with the cursor.

Or, you can drop down and click on **Advanced Font Options** to open the dropdown list and click on the far-right button (the large A with the curved arrow and small a). There will be a dropdown from this, which you can use to click on **UPPER CASE**. And again, if you don't have any text highlighted this will be grayed out, so go back and highlight text if this is the case. So, you do have some options in Kindle Create, a little flexibility. Not a lot, but I'm sure with time Amazon will increase the number of bells and whistles, and improve the software. And I'm just guessing here, but there might just come a time when Amazon will decide that the KC program is the only option they want to allow. Like I said, I'm just guessing. If so, hopefully it has a lot more functionality by then.

In any case, you will be way ahead of the game, because you will already know how to use it.

In any event, as with most any word processing software, you can go through your document and edit things here in this KC software. Basic stuff. Perhaps you see that there is a spelling error. They always get through; I don't know how, but they do. It seems like it doesn't matter how many times you edit your work, or have it edited, proofread, etc. Some errors always slip through. Just try to catch as many as you can.

This is why I will usually publish the ebook first and then read through it in the kindle software to look for errors. Then I'll highlight the errors. Just color them a bright yellow, as though you are simply highlighting a line of text that you like. You don't like these errors, of course. Highlighting them here means that all you do is sit down at your computer with the tablet in your lap. You have your book open in kindle, and your book opened on the computer (the Word document) for editing. You will, of course, have to edit your book in both files: The Word file (paperback) and the Kindle Create file.

That is the only drawback of using both to publish. However, it is a minor issue; at least in my opinion.

And, I believe you would have to update two files in any case . . .

And now, here's another little tidbit for KC: suppose you have a webpage and want to **add a clickable link** that will take the reader to your webpage. This can be in the back matter, or wherever. Well, to set this up in Kindle Create, this is what you do:

Type something like **Contact Me at** and then select the words to highlight them with the cursor. Then go up to the left-hand top of the screen where you can click on the plus sign + **Insert** button, which is right next to the magnifying glass "Find" symbol. A list will open up and you can go down and click where it says **Hyperlink**. A dialog box will open up where you can type or copy and paste in the link to your webpage. Then just click **Insert Hyperlink** to complete the process. That's all there is to it.

Now, you have your book in Kindle Create and you believe you have everything exactly like you want it. Now you want to view the book in the previewer to see what your masterpiece will actually look like on someone's device.

Go up and click on the **Preview** button in the upper right-hand corner. This button is right between the **Save** button and the **Publish** button.

Just a Note:

In places in your book, there will be wide gaps of space between words sometimes. This will look like the software sort of stretching the sentence across the width of the page. Most times there is nothing you can do about this. I wouldn't worry too much about it. Fix what you can and hope for the best regarding what you have no control over—that's my motto.

You will also notice in KC that there is a **Theme** button in the upper right area of the screen. You have three different options. You can check the different options out and decide. I usually just use the Classic theme.

I went up and checked them out with my example manuscript just now and I don't know if that is what caused my chapter/story titles to shift to the left, but I had to go through and center them all again by highlighting each one and then going to the Paragraph section under the formatting heading and then click on the second icon. It is very similar to the option in Word's Home screen.

And there is, in fact, a tab for header titles and page numbers. I have never paid any attention to it before. I have always just left the setting on whatever its default setting is. However, I guess this means you can change it if you want, move the text of heading to middle or side of the page, or whatever. The only strange part is that the option is for paperback. And as far as I know, you can't do a paperback from this file. Maybe Amazon is just planning ahead . . . or maybe I'm wrong. I'll have to look next time I go on KDP.

An Update!

With the newest download of Kindle Create software there is an option for you to try a beta version which offers paperback formatting, so it is in the works.

The software overall, however, is so limited, at least for now, that I would stick to Word. Supposedly, you can upload a Word file (doc or docx) to the Amazon site for ebooks, but I didn't have a tremendous amount of success with it initially. That was early on though in the process. I might have been doing something wrong. Maybe I should try again. However, I've gotten so used to using KC for the upload vehicle that I'll probably just continue to use it, at least for now.

KC works fantastic as the upload vehicle. I know everything is going to go super smooth. I can preview everything and see exactly how it is going to look in the little previewer, and even click on the link to my website and go right to it from the previewer.

And so now . . .

Once you have everything exactly like you want it, and your manuscript looks good in the previewer, then you can click on the publish button.

To Publish, just click on the **Publish** icon in the upper far right corner (right next to the Preview button. The important thing to remember here is that this doesn't mean you are publishing to Amazon when you click this button. All this does is format a file that will be stored on your hard drive that will be ready for uploading to Amazon whenever you get ready. This file used to be sort of an ugly brown looking file (It looked like a brown, corrugated cardboard folder—that's the only way I know how to describe it). They have since changed the look of the file—Now it is a standard White "K" in a blue circle. On the one hand, I sort of miss the ugly brown file as it was really easy to spot when it came time for upload. But you just have to look for the blue circle with the K and the file extension/type of **KPF**. You can place this file anywhere you want. When you click the publish button and things proceed, you will be asked if you want to show the KC file. Click yes. Now you are all set. Close out. Done. When you are on the Amazon dashboard, and are publishing your ebook; when you click on the **upload your manuscript file** button, just look for the K file and upload it. There will be absolutely no problems. Amazon will accept this little file that holds your beautiful manuscript. You will have a published ebook. Well, provided you go through and fill out all the rest of the information, upload the cover, etc.

To Prepare/Publish your Paperback

Okay, so now back to the main file that you have gotten ready for your paperback. You have checked it all over and then added drop caps or any other fancy features you wanted to add. The rest is simple. You'll just have to go export the file to a pdf document format.

Open the file in Word, then
Go to/click on **File**
Click on **Export** (just above the **close** near the bottom of the list.

Create PDF/XPS Document should be highlighted. Just go over and click on the icon.
After clicking on Create PDF button, a window will open and the name of the file will be highlighted. Below this, look for the **Optimize for: Standard** (Publishing online and printing). This radio button should be checked.

Click on **Options**
All radio button should be ticked.

Document radio button should be ticked
PDF Options should be set to **PDF/A Compliant**
Click on **OK** button.
Click **Publish**

It might take a couple of minutes, but a PDF document will open for you to look over. If it doesn't, then you didn't have the box checked to show or open the document in the options section (I believe).

Read over the PDF. Scroll all the way through this document. This is your book. Look, again for headings, page numbers, etc. Make sure everything looks as it is all supposed to. You should be used to checking things over, looking for the same things over and over. You know what to check for now.

And when you close out, the PDF document will be on your hard drive, ready to upload to Amazon whenever you are ready to create the paperback on your Amazon KDP dashboard.

Okay, so the only thing, or question is what to do when Amazon assigns you your ISBN? You want it in the printed book, right?

So when they assign it you can copy it down (or right click and copy) then go to your copyright page in the Word document for your book and type (or copy) it in beneath the copyright info. The only problem is that now you will have to export the PDF again. Just save it with the same name. You will be asked if you want to overwrite the file with the same name. Click Yes. Then upload the file. The only way around this is to not create the PDF file until after they assign you the number. Which maybe they do assign it near the beginning of the publishing process, before you come to the part about uploading your manuscript. That would make more sense. I just always have the pdf ready before I even go to kdp. And maybe you can even type it right into the pdf file. I'll have to check on it. I always just minimize the window. Then maximize the Word file and type the isbn right there on the copyright page and then save and export the file as a pdf again with the same name and stored in the same folder. Then I simply maximize the Amazon kdp window again and click the upload button.

When the question arises about the ISBN, of course, you might have already purchased your own ISBN from Bowker. And that is a whole different ballgame. I have never done that. I just use the Amazon assigned ASIN or ISBN. I type it in the book as ISBN-13: *insert the number here.*

If you create a new file folder with the book title as the file name, and keep it right on your desktop, then you can store everything there relating to your novel/book:

Your paperback PDF file.

Your KC files (for your ebook).

And your initial Word file, along with your cover jpeg file, and everything else. Uploading the cover for the ebook is pretty basic—you just upload a photo/jpg file (I believe there might also be an option for a **png** file though I've never used it.

***

A Note on uploading to Amazon:

The last book I published (under a pseudonym in November 2022) I had trouble getting the book to upload. Trying to get it uploaded took about seven tries. I kept thinking that I was doing something wrong. I checked things over several times. Each time I tried to upload the PDF file I would get an error. It was around 3:00 a.m. and I finally gave up and went to bed. The next day (actually it was later the same day, after I had gotten some sleep) the book uploaded just fine on the first try.

So what had been the problem?

Nothing on my side.

Unfortunately, if things are busy on Amazon's side, they will only let you try to upload a manuscript a couple of times. Perhaps as many as three.

This was news to me. I believe I read it in some fine print on the KDP site. Or perhaps I had Googled it. I don't remember. It would be nice if they presented a message box on your last chance to try. I was going nuts double checking everything. I couldn't figure out why I kept getting an error. This was the nineteenth book I was publishing. This was the first time this had ever happened to me. All eighteen previous books had worked. When I got an error any previous time it was due to some error I had made. This one wasn't on me, but I thought it must have been at the time.

So, if you keep getting errors when you try to upload, and you know that you have done everything correctly, just walk away and come back to try a couple of hours later. You will be successful at some point. You'll eventually be able to upload your book for publication.

Don't get discouraged!

Notes on Cover creation/upload, etc.

Now, the cover for the paperback is a little more complex. Hopefully, you've gotten a cover done at fiverr or on 99designs, or CANVA. Or you might even decide to use the amazon cover creator. People say don't use it, but I have used it for one nonfiction book I put up under a pseudonym and it worked just fine. I have used all of the above except CANVA. As of this writing, I have a couple of covers up that I created myself, and at least one that looks awful. I will change it soon. If you feel that your skills are up to par with photoshop or whatever, then go for it. Bad idea, and everyone advises against doing it yourself. But I've still tried it, mainly due to frustration at trying to find someone else to do a cover properly. My skills were very rusty, and I never was a great graphic artist anyway. However, I've since bought a digital tablet, practiced brushing up my Photoshop skills and done several of my own covers (as of the updating of this book). *The Red Kimono* is one of the covers I am most proud of having done. I designed the cover in photoshop. It took three to five hours of work, and then praying that I would be allowed to use the photo I had downloaded from Kim + Ono. They were kind enough to allow it. You can see this cover and all the others at

www.markstattelman.com

if you are interested.

On my civil war dark tale series, I had someone on fiverr do the first two covers (the second one I had to take the photo of a Halloween wolf and then upload it for the designer to use). Since then, I've used those two covers as templates to do the rest of the covers in the series. I just change out the title and the other information in photoshop. It is a grueling process, even just doing that.

You can look at the cover from 99designs for my non-fiction book **Write Play Love**, and see how much more professional it looks. You can see the cover on my site also.

Covers and editing are the most expensive part of the book publishing process. It is advisable to pay what you can afford for a cover.

99designs, if you aren't familiar with it, is a site where designers from all over the world submit designs to you and then you decide. It is quite overwhelming. I believe I had 107 designs to choose from at one point for the Write Play Love book. The base price was $299 to start the contest. I believe I paid another $25 for something up front (I just can't remember what it was for). And of course, if the art-work/photo is not free and open copyright, then you might have to pay a little more for that. It usually isn't too much. I believe mine was free. I had such a difficult time deciding on a cover, that I went to another site called pickfu to get votes on eight designs. You can only submit eight photos I believe. Or perhaps it was just the plan I signed up for. In any case it was market research: 50 strangers chose my cover. I probably would have gone with a black one that looked almost identical to the white; but in the end I chose to trust the research since I had paid for it. The black cover came in third. I believe you can see some of these covers as examples of work on the site (99designs not pickfu). If you google my name, often times the covers from the 99design contest show up. You have the option of checking a box when you set up the contest to have it all visible to the public.

Sorry about going into all of that, since this is a book on formatting, not cover design issues, but I thought you might need to know some of it for general information. Getting covers done, for me at least, has been the most difficult part.

Fiverr is hit or miss. You can sometimes get decent covers, and sometimes not.

Just know, also, that you will have to convert the cover jpeg to a pdf file for uploading to Amazon. If you have windows 10 you can do it yourself, don't pay anyone, or buy any special software.

The person who does your book cover for ebook (which is just a front cover jpg) and paperback cover will almost assuredly send the paperback cover to you in pdf format in any case. If for some reason they don't, this is what you do (along with getting your money back from a designer who doesn't know what they're doing) to turn a jpg file into a pdf file:

Click on window Icon in bottom left corner of screen to bring up program list.

Go to **photos** (with jagged mountain outline) not the same as picture Click to open

Look at top right of screen once the program opens and select import **from a folder** or **from a USB device**

For some reason the from a folder choice never works for me. I usually am bringing the photo in from another computer anyway after saving it into a jpg file in photoshop. So I use USB.

This program is a HUGE pain in the rear and will not let you just grab a single jpg file from your desktop or wherever. Every time I've clicked on Import file nothing happens. And apparently, they want you to import a whole file of photos anyway.

However, if you do manage to get a photo into this program, then (and maybe I'm just ignorant as far as how to use it.) this is what you do in order to turn a photo/book cover jpg file into a pdf file:

Select the photo (by ticking the box in the upper right of the photo image), and then go up and click on the printer Icon (or use Ctrl +P). A box should open up with the name of your printer. There should be a dropdown arrow, use this dropdown arrow to then select **Microsoft Print to PDF.**

Decide on your settings and then choose Print.

Then decide on where you want to store the file and what you want to name it and click **Save**. The last part is pretty basic.

Don't know why they had to make things so unnecessarily difficult . . .

And like I said, your cover design person will send you the photo pdf file for your paperback cover. So, you will probably never have to use this. Since I mentioned this earlier, I thought I should clue you in.

I've had to use it once or twice, as I've changed things on a cover template in photoshop and then had to figure out how to turn the jpg file into a pdf file in order to upload the cover to Amazon.

Anyway, this book is about how to format the inside of your manuscript—so anything else I give you is just extraneous, I guess, so you can ignore it if you want.

Streamlining and Automating:

OK. Honestly, I'm not sure how helpful this section really is—at least with regard to Templates.

When I first wrote this section, I thought that setting up a template would be extremely helpful. However, when I went to format my next book there still seemed to be too much work involved.

Let me explain. I thought that a template would be awesome. I would be able to simply type in my title, headers, footers, etc. And I expected all of the margins, trim size, fonts, etc. would remain set . . .

For the most part this is true.

As I realized, however, the template seemed not a lot different than my copying one of my previously formatted manuscripts and then deleting out the earlier information and typing or copying in the new info.

The only difference with a template it seems is that the template can't be accidentally deleted by accident, whereas just a copy of an earlier manuscript can be deleted easily.

That's it! That seems to be the only difference. And maybe I'm simply not understanding exactly how templates are supposed to work.

In any case, I, as of this update to the book (June 2023) have decided to leave this section in the book. I thought about removing the section, but then decided against this. Some of you, might still find the information useful. Perhaps it's just my not understanding things. Perhaps some of you can find ways to improve on the process. If so, I hope to hear from you. In which case I'll make the needed corrections. A better plan might be to simply modify, or add a new style in the styles section to work with. I'm guessing you will be able to then just reuse that Style each time you write a new book.

***

So, here is the Template section as I initially wrote it, either originally or in the first update of the book:

Now that you've done all the work of creating your first book, you don't want to have to go through it all again for the next book. Make things easy on yourself by creating a template. After all, wouldn't it be nice if all you had to do for your next book is open up a document that is already formatted exactly how you like it, including headers and footers (page numbers), etc.? Here's how you do that.

Create a Template:

Make a copy of your manuscript from the "Clean copy." You can do this if you have the file open by going to **File**, then clicking on **Save As**. Change the name to something like **My Book Template**, or whatever you want to call it. Don't change the file type just yet. Leave it as a regular word document for now.

If the file is closed, you can do this by locating the copy on your desktop (or wherever you have it stored). Right-Click on the file and click on Copy. Move cursor to wherever you want the new file and Right-Click again and click on Paste. Next, Right-Click on this copy and click on Rename. Type the new name and press enter. Then open the file.

Now if you have the file open, at the top of the screen you should see the new name of My Book Template or whatever you chose to name it. On the **Home** tab on the blue ribbon, go to the **Paragraph** section and click on the backwards P in the upper right corner. As you should know by now, this makes all of the hidden punctuation symbols visible. We are doing this because we are going to delete out most of the content (if not all) of each of your chapters and we want to make sure that we don't delete out the section breaks at the end of each chapter. Sad, I know. You've worked so hard on your manuscript, but hey, we made this copy, right? You still have the original "Clean copy."

At this point you can go ahead and highlight everything from, or starting with Chapter Two on back to the end of the book and then hit the delete key. You can stop just before the backmatter if you want. So you will just still have the Afterward, etc. This backmatter will just be up behind Chapter One. All we are doing here is making sure that we have enough of the properly formatted section of the book still intact.

Go to your **Title page**. Highlight the Title and simply type **TITLE**. Do the same thing on the Half Title page (if you have one). Go to subtitle, highlight it and type the word Subtitle. You obviously won't have to change the author name unless you are going to write your next book under a pseudonym.

You can pretty much leave all of the frontmatter as is. Of course, you could go through and just leave the title words, like **Dedication,** but do keep the titles. Don't delete any pages. You want to keep all of the formatting setup like you've got it. Leave Copyright page, etc. Though you might want to delete out the ISBN number and just leave the "ISBN:" in place.

Your Table of Contents page should now just be showing the first couple of chapters. It should have updated automatically. This is fine.

Now **go to the First chapter** (which should be the only chapter you have) and delete out the content from the second line all the way back to the backwards paragraph symbol and the dotted line that reads Section Break. Make sure to keep this line. It should just now be moved up to first page of the chapter. Obviously, you are trying to keep the formatting in place.

Remember the trouble you went through to remove the page numbers and headers on the first page. You can experiment if you want and see how much content you can get by with deleting on the first page. You can also change the text that you keep to just say something generic, like *this is text*, or maybe just type all 'x's or whatever.

Now, if you type in content (or copy it in), you should still have headers and page numbers intact. **Move cursor to top margin and double click** to bring up header. **Highlight** the book title (which should be on the odd pages still) and type something generic, like **Book Title**, or **My Book**. You get the idea. You won't have to change the author name, of course, because it will be you writing the next book.

If you might want to use a pseudonym, but haven't decided yet, then you can also change this to something generic, like **Author Name**.

Once you have everything whittled down and changed whatever is left to just generic type stuff, you can go ahead and save it as a template. I'll tell you how to do this in a minute.

In any case, the next book you write, you'll just have to highlight and change the generic info to whatever the new book is about. Change headings accordingly, etc.

I did just try this, copying and pasting in a story. The font type, style and other formatting didn't hold quite as planned. Of course, that might have been where I clicked the "paste-keep formatting" instead of the "paste-merge formatting." Also, had I set up the **Normal** *Style* on the Styles Tab to permanently hold my desired settings, the font and line spacing, etc. would have probably held. Like I said, I have a tendency to just right-click and modify the Normal Style temporarily. The Headers held, and also the settings for chapter/story title page (no header on top, or page # on bottom of first page of chapter/story). That's the main thing, because it is the most difficult to fool with. It's all a little messy, but still beats going back to step one every time. You can get a feel for it and figure out what works best for you and your style of writing.

I believe that had I simply typed out a chapter/story in the template (to then be saved as a Word doc) all the fonts and everything would have remained consistent with what I wanted. When I typed it all earlier it seemed to hold up.

Most people will, in fact, have the template set up on the computer that they do their writing on, typing directly into the document. I'm still caught up on writing out my stories on an older laptop with Word 2000 and then saving to thumb drive for the transfer to the newer system/version, copying and pasting. It is just what I'm used to. I'll probably not switch over until the old laptop dies.

And so now, to save as a template . . .

To Save as a Template:

Go to **File**

Click on **Save As**

Decide where you want to save the file. Let's choose the desktop for now so you can see what the file looks like. If you have a Books file folder on your desktop in which you keep all of your works in progress that would be convenient.

Leave the name if you changed it to **My Book Template** (or whatever) earlier.

Click the drop-down arrow of the **Save As Type** box and then find and choose **Word Template** from the list. This should be about the fourth down in the list. Normally you would save your work as a Word Document. Not this time.

Click Save.

Now, close out of the file. Find it on your desktop. See how it looks different than a regular Word file. It has a strip along the top, looking very much like a note pad of paper; You know the kind that you would write a grocery list on and then rip the top sheet off

Okay, now Open Word again and click on **File**. You should see your file in the section that shows all of the pre-made Word templates. If you don't see it there then click on *more templates* on the far right with the arrow. You'll see two sections: **Office** and **Personal**. Your Template should be showing in Personal. If you click on the template it should open properly. Don't open it there, however. Instead, go back to the desktop. Click on this file on the desktop to open it. If you look at the top of the window when it opens, you'll see that this file is a regular Word document, exactly as if you opened a new blank document in Word. You would now save this document as you would a regular Word file, as it is only a copy of the Template you just created: When you get ready to close out of the file you can save it with whatever name you want, such as My New Book (or the new book's title).

Now, suppose later on you decide you want to change something in the Template that you've created. Let's suppose you want to streamline it a little more, or you decide to change to a new font or whatever. You would be able to do this in your regular Word document file that you've started based on the template. You can change all kinds of things and save the document. However, when you open the template to start another book, you will have to start again with the settings that you set up in the original template. So, to edit the template you'll have to do something else.

Edit and Resave as a Template:

If you want to change or edit something in your template, you won't be able to save it under the original name. The original Template is still in existence. You will have to name it something else and then go and delete the original if you no longer want it. It's okay to change things, but basically, you're simply creating a whole new Template. You can go and delete the original template and then rename this one if you want, giving this Template the original name. Up to you. Or you can delete the original before saving this document as a template.

To Delete a Template:

The brief version:

Click on Windows Icon in bottom left corner of the screen (of Windows 10). On the task bar. Same place you would go to shut down the computer.
Click on document Icon on left, "quick menu" (I believe that's what it's called). The document icon is the one that looks like a page with the upper right corner bent down. And it even says Documents, strangely enough.

Look for the folder titled **Custom Office Templates.** It should be in the left-hand "Quick Access" list. If not, go down and click on This Computer. The folder should then show in the right-hand pane.
Click to **open** the Custom Office Templates folder.
You should then see your template, the one you want to delete.
Right-Click and **delete** the template file.

As you can tell, Microsoft doesn't make it too easy for you to delete your template. That is as it should be, I guess. You want that stability. The only time it's a hassle is when you decide you don't need it anymore and want to get rid of it. So close out of everything, and then open Word again and **click New**, as though you want to start a writing project. Guess what? There it is. If it isn't there, then go to the right-hand side of the string of Templates where it says more templates and there is an arrow pointing right. Click on this to open up another section. If you still don't see it, look below to where it says **Office**, and then **Personal**. Click on Personal. There it is, right? You might have seen it listed earlier in the New section, and also here. If you see the file now, click on it. What is the message? Something indicating that the file couldn't be found. Now you can safely and easily right-click and get rid of this non-existent file. You can't even hit delete now. It says **Remove from list**. Do this. Had you gone straight to this section before and tried to delete, you wouldn't have been able to delete it.

Try this as an experiment:

Open a New Blank document. Type FAKE TEM-PLATE. You can center the words and click Title in the Styles section on Home tab selection. Close out this file, saving it as **Fake Template** and saving the **Save as Type: Word Template**. As far as place to save it, Click on Desktop and Custom Office Template file folder. Save it there.

Now Open Word if it is not already open. I'm not sure if you have to close Word and then re-open it to get it to show. Click on File New There it is, your Fake Template. It is probably somewhere in the list with, and near, the Blank document; And it is probably also down beneath the Personal heading. Try right-clicking on the file to delete it. The only options are to "Create, or Pin to list" right? Delete isn't even listed. So go ahead and just close out and then do as we just did earlier: hit the Windows Icon in the left bottom corner, click Documents, and find the Custom Office Templates folder. Open the folder and right-click to delete the Fake Template. Then go back up and 'Remove" the thumbnail that has the Fake Template name.

And so that's it, you now have a **template** that you can open up and use for your next book. I'm quite sure there is a more formal way to set up a real template. There is something called "Bit Parts, or Part Bits. And if you have activated the Developer tab there is even a Document Template tab in that section. This, of course, is getting into deeper waters than I intended to go. I'll have to explore it all a bit more. Perhaps in a later edition of the book I'll go there. For now, however, messy as it seems, you can probably get by well enough with the make-shift template for now. If you want to explore all of it a little more, then great. You can show me how to do it!

There are probably more things you can do to streamline the whole process overall, and make each successive book easier to set up and write, etc. And then, of course, with a little time and effort you'll be formatting books left and right and won't have to depend on anyone.

Just remember when formatting in Word, if things get screwy it is probably due to not having a **section break** after a chapter, or not having something unlinked. The **Link to Previous** button will be the bane of your formatting life—at least until you master it. So Master it!

Play around. If you are uncomfortable using your own text, then download a book from the Gutenberg Project and play with the formatting. Cut and paste this into your newly created Template

I realize that a lot of this stuff is overwhelming; As is anything when you are first trying to learn it. A little effort and flexibility will get you there. Just follow the guidelines I've laid out here for a good start. My intent here was just to get you up and running. I didn't want you to have to go through all the trouble I went through when I first started and had to figure it all out.

Other Options/Other File Formats

I know that I said I wouldn't discuss things I haven't actually used. But here goes . . .

I figure I should at least mention a few other formatting options to explore. Once you have your Word document in pristine condition you might decide that you want to change your Word document to another format. We've already covered converting the document to a PDF, but there are many other options, and several other platforms besides Amazon. You can upload your document to a site called

Draft to Digital, a.k.a. D2D

and get them to convert your file. They will do this for free, whether you publish with them or not. I've tried this option, and it does work. I'm still trying to figure it all out. D2D is a wide distributor. If your book is not in the Kindle Select Program then you are not locked into Amazon solely. You can publish your ebook through D2D and have it distributed to Apple, Barnes and Noble, and many other places worldwide in the various formats required: epub, Kobo, Mobi (which is Amazon's format—to whom D2D also distributes if you aren't already published directly with Amazon).

Once I become more familiar with this D2D path I will be able to give you more information by updating this book. From what I've done so far with D2D it was fairly easy to use, and I was happy with it. There is just so much there that it is a little overwhelming. I did do a blog post about my experiences which you can check out here:

https://markstattelman.com/loving-draft2digital/

Of course, you can explore this option on your own. I'm just giving you a heads up that this is another platform/option. And of course, I've mentioned the free conversion option.

Calibre, etc.

Calibre is free software that you can download to your computer and you can use it to convert your Word document to PDF, epub, Mobi, and a whole slew of the other format types. I have played around with this software some and hope to spend even more time playing around with it.

Calibre is extremely intuitive and easy to use. There is an ereader, and you can use it to store a whole library of digital books. You can use it to search for metadata for any published book: Your own, etc. There are a whole lot of features here. I have experimented with the conversion aspect. Inevitably the conversion from one format to another is not perfect. You will have to watch closely. I have changed my own books into various other of the more common formats. And I have also downloaded free books from The Gutenberg Project to play around with. I suggest trying this. I usually download the epub version and then convert it into a Word document, or a PDF. I have found that if a book has any sort of Drama, or poetry type structure, or formatted columns similar to a newspaper, it gets extremely jumbled if converting directly to a Word document from epub. Often times the original formatting of this type holds together a little better by converting first to PDF, and then from PDF to Word. I'll have to double check this, and play around a little more. It is possible that one of the other formats that I haven't a clue about, and have never heard of, might do a better job. So stay tuned. Or better yet, download this free software for yourself and play around. It is fun experimenting with it and changing or converting to different file formats, etc. just to see what happens.

There is also something called SmashWords. I am completely unfamiliar with it, however. I believe it is simply another publishing platform, etc. There are several more.

I will stop here, however, since this is a book about formatting for Amazon using MS Word, and I've already stepped further outside of the bounds than I initially intended.

This is just a fascinating time to be alive and be an independent, or "Indie" author. The traditional way of book publishing has been completely upended, and things are changing fast. The stigma that once surrounded a self-published author is starting to fade away. This hasn't gone completely away, but the wall is crumbling.

So, write that book, format it, get it edited, proofread, get the cover and then upload it all. Of course, that's when the real work starts-marketing! And yes, you have to do it all. Or not. Hire out what you *have to*, but formatting shouldn't be one of the jobs you pay someone else to do. You'll be paying out the nose over the long haul if you do. And now that you know how to do the formatting yourself . . . well, you're good to go.

Thank You for Reading this book. I sincerely hope it helps you. I plan to do a little more research and playing around with things. And perhaps the next edition will be even more helpful.

If this book did help you then please feel free to leave a review on Amazon. Others might need the help too, but won't be sure if this is the right book for them unless you leave a review saying how helpful it is.

Also, if you don't feel it is helpful, then help me to make it better:

Contact me at www.markstattelman.com

Or at markstattelman@gmail.com

You can also catch me on **Goodreads.com** which is one of my favorite hangouts. It's free and fun. Join me there and feel free to *Friend* me, *Follow* me, or whatever.

Thanks Again!

Also, just a note: If you want to do things the old-fashioned way by submitting a formatted hardcopy to a publisher, do an internet search for a guy by the name of William Shunn. He has a list of guidelines and also templates for both short story and novel. I found him by way of Ellery Queen's Mystery magazine, or Asimov's Science Fiction magazine. (same owner). One of them had a link to this guy for their submission guidelines, so he is legit.

Mark Stattelman

Author

Thriller, Mystery, Suspense, Horror, Sci-Fi, Historical Fiction

https://www.markstattelman.com

And nonfiction, of course!

Printed in Great Britain
by Amazon

33022926R00076